ST AUSTELL
The Golden Years

ST AUSTELL
The Golden Years

THE TOWN AND CLAY COUNTRY DURING THE 1950S AND 1960S

Peter Hancock

with additional photographs by
John Smith

First published in Great Britain in 2004

Copyright © 2004 Peter Hancock
Copyright © on images in Chapter Nine, John Smith

All rights reserved. No part of this publication may be reproduced, stored in a retrieval system, or transmitted in any form or by any means without the prior permission of the copyright holder.

British Library Cataloguing-in-Publication Data
A CIP record for this title is available from the British Library

ISBN 1 84114 388 X

HALSGROVE

Halsgrove House
Lower Moor Way
Tiverton, Devon EX16 6SS
Tel: 01884 243242
Fax: 01884 243325
email: sales@halsgrove.com
website: www.halsgrove.com

Printed and bound in Great Britain
by CPI, Bath

CONTENTS

	Acknowledgements	6
	Introduction	7
1	The Town	9
2	Local Businesses	21
3	Around the Coast	33
4	Changing Schools	49
5	At Work	55
6	Sport	69
7	Happy Days	85
8	The Clay Country and Hinterland	103
9	One Christmas Eve...	121

ACKNOWLEDGEMENTS

I wish to thank the following for providing photographs and information: Mr P. Barbery; Mr R. Bassett (MB); Mr J. Smith; Mrs M. Bath (MB); Mr I. Bowditch of Imerys Minerals Ltd (IM); Mr R. Boundy (RBO); Mr P. Browning; the *Cornish Guardian* (CGU); The Cornwall Centre, Redruth; Cornwall County Fire Brigade St Austell (CCFB); Mr A. Deller (AD); Mr S. Edyvean; Mr and Mrs L. Ford; Mr and Mrs W.A. Frazier (WAF); Mrs M. Godwin (MG); Mrs G. Gribble (GG); Dr J. Hancock; Mr E. Jamilly, Dip.Arch RIBA ACArch; Mr T. Langson (TL); Mid Cornwall Photographic Services (MCPS); the staff and trustees of Mevagissey Museum (MMU); Mr and Mrs M. Opie (MO); Mr B. Powell; Mr C. Roberts; the staff at St Austell Library; Mr H. Pryce (HP); Mr and Mrs R. Sandercock (RS); Mrs B. Snell (BS); Mr J. Stephens (JS); Mrs M. Stephens; Mr D. Stone (DS); Mr I. Toms (IT); Wheal Martyn China Clay Museum's Curator, Miss E. Chard and Mr B. Strathen, Collections Assistant (WHM); and Mrs J. Wilcocks (JW). Press photographs taken by George Ellis (GE) are also included. Thanks are also due to Mr S. Butler of Halsgrove who proposed the idea in the first place.

Without their generous assistance this book would not have come into existence.

Every effort has been made to obtain permission to reproduce the images included here, but if there have been any omissions, the author and publisher apologise unreservedly.

INTRODUCTION

In many ways the 1950s and '60s were 'Golden Years'. After the trauma and hardships suffered during the war, people were getting their lives back to normal and looking forward to a better future. This optimism was reflected in the Festival of Britain in May 1951. Nevertheless, the country was still haunted by the past. Rationing on many commodities continued into the 1950s, and in some instances grew worse. Then, during the Suez Crisis in July 1956, petrol rationing even returned for a short time.

The death of George VI in February 1952 and the subsequent coronation of his daughter in June 1953 heralded a new Elizabethan age. There was an increase in prosperity to the point where, by July 1957, Prime Minister Harold Macmillan was able to announce 'Indeed, let us be frank about it: most of our people have never had it so good.' Consumerism increased, along with people's expectations and aspirations in what was to be dubbed the 'Swinging Sixties'. The country was on a high, and during a time of 'Export or Die' it was the centre for industrial manufacturing, as well as a world leader in art, fashion and pop culture. Then, to cap it all, in 1966 England won the World Cup.

Not that the period was free of disasters, including the tragedy at Aberfan in 1966 and the loss of the *Torrey Canyon*. On the world stage the decade was marred by civil unrest and the Vietnam War.

St Austell might not have been at the forefront of these events, but their effects were often felt and assimilated by the residents of this growing market town – St Austell Brewery organised a trip for its employees to the Festival of Britain; petrol rationing threatened the tourist industry during the spring and early summer of 1956; carnival floats in August 1963 claimed to be carrying some of the Great Train Robbers; the tourist industry was again threatened in March 1967 by the stranding of the *Torrey Canyon* on the Seven Stones Reef off the Isles of Scilly, while technicians at E.C.L.P.'s (English Clays Lovering Pochin & Co.) laboratories were busy experimenting with sand as a way of sinking the oil.

Whilst researching this book I met many interesting people who shared with me wonderful recollections of the time. However, one overriding opinion came across – the period of the 1950s and '60s was one of different values, aspirations and interests, when people were content with simple pleasures. Large crowds attended local football matches or speedway events. St Austell residents took pride in their town – both the old part and the new modern town centre – and its local businesses. The population was that much smaller before large housing estates were built, and a community spirit prevailed within the town and the china clay district.

The photographs in this book come from a wide range of sources, so it is inevitable that the quality of the images vary. They include items reproduced from treasured photograph albums, snaps exumed from the back of dusty drawers, old postcards, images stored in museums, and press photographs including those taken by George Ellis. They have been supplemented by advertisements, programmes and posters of the period which, I feel, help to give a true sense of St Austell and the china-clay district during these 'Golden Years'.

An aerial view of the town centre at the start of our period. The church can be seen at the top of the photograph, Fore Street curves towards the bottom left and South Street towards the bottom right. The photograph pre-dates the construction of the town centre or Trinity Street. (IT)

Chapter One
THE TOWN

The official opening of Trinity Street on 27 July 1962. Mr J.C. Wakeford, Chairman of St Austell Urban District Council, is seen unveiling the new name. (GE)

Mr Wakeford and his wife taking the first walk down the street which would provide a valuable link between South Street and the Fore Street/Truro Road/West Hill/Bodmin Road junction. (GE)

An aerial photograph, taken postwar, looking north-west across the town towards Trenance viaduct. In the foreground can be seen Pentewan Road roundabout, and the old gasometers to the left of Moorland Road. In the centre is West Hill School, and open ground occupies the area that was later developed as the town centre. The large white building to the right is the Odeon Cinema.

THE TOWN

Key to Drawing:

1 Gasometers, made redundant with the introduction of natural gas and removed in the late 1960s.

2 John Williams' buildings, replaced by a B&Q store and car parks.

3 Site of Park House flats, built in the late 1960s.

4 West Hill School, latterly an annex of Mid-Cornwall Technical College, was demolished in 1999 and the site developed for the College Green/Trinity Street housing scheme. The playing-field had already been used for the site of a new tax office in 1992.

5 Sedgemoor Hotel, which stands derelict in 2003.

6 Public Rooms, now Courts furniture showrooms.

7 Car park and surrounding open ground used for Trinity Street and the new town centre.

8 St John's Methodist Chapel which celebrated its 175th anniversary in June 2003.

9 The Fire Station. Its inconvenient position at Bodmin Road met with widespread criticism and it was replaced by a new facility at Polkyth in 2003.

10 The Trenance branch line to Carthew that had opened in 1920 was closed around 1962.

11 The Odeon Cinema, now the film centre boasting five screens. It is likely to be demolished during the early-twenty-first century as part of the £40 million new town centre redevelopment scheme.

12 The Workhouse, demolished to make way for the Sedgemoor Campus of St Austell College.

13 The Congregational Chapel was demolished and the site used for the Royal British Legion Club and a garden.

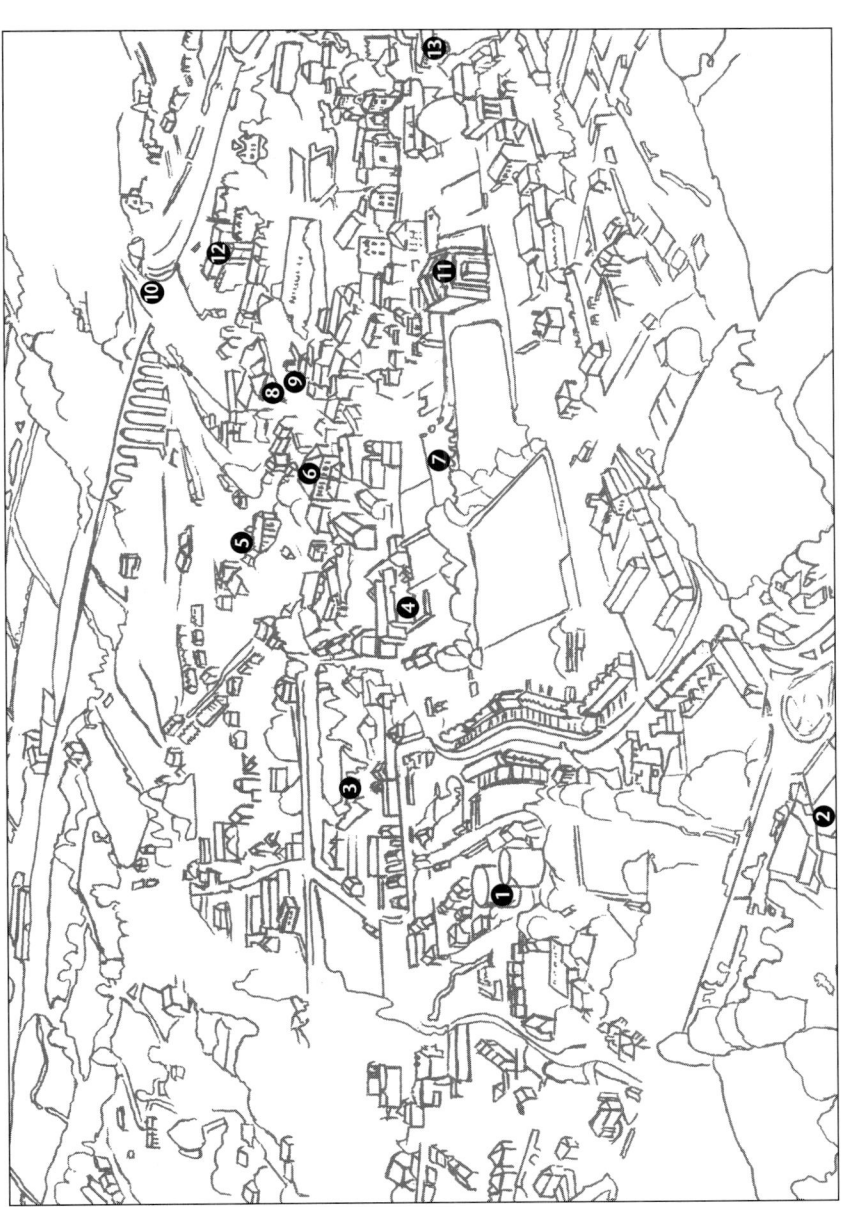

ST AUSTELL – *The Golden Years*

St Austell's public library just being completed in March 1961. The new building replaced the old library in Victoria Square and was subsequently extended to provide a specialist Performing Arts and Music department. It is now listed. (GE)

The Society of Friends' (Quakers) burial-ground at Tregongeeves being removed for a new road-widening scheme, 20 February 1965. The site had served the local Quaker community since 1664. It is now marked with a slate plaque next to the busy A390 to Truro. (GE)

THE TOWN

The new Church Hall, with the railway-yard buildings in the background, 11 June 1960. (GE)

The proposed new town centre, as illustrated in a booklet of street maps of St Austell, Par and Fowey issued by the estate agents, May, Whetter & Grose. The final version of the development was somewhat more prosaic.

ST AUSTELL – *The Golden Years*

ST. AUSTELL'S GROWING NEW TOWN CENTRE

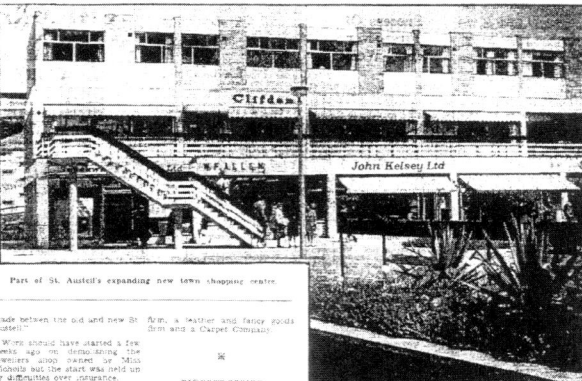

Part of St. Austell's expanding new town shopping centre.

St Austell's new town centre is the subject of a half-page advert in the *Cornish Guardian* of 11 May 1967.

W.F. Allen found premises for their jewellery business in the new town centre. This advert appeared in the *Cornish Guardian* on 31 August 1967.

Getting engaged?

Only your diamond ring captures and holds this wonderful moment throughout your life together.
We have a beautiful selection of diamond engagement rings and will be glad to give you helpful advice in choosing your ring.

a diamond is forever

W. F. ALLEN
(JEWELLERS) LTD.
New Town Centre
ST. AUSTELL
Telephone : ST. AUSTELL 3104

THE TOWN

A bobby looks on as a new Oxfam shop is opened in Duke Street in 1968. The guest of honour, BBC news reader Joe Pengelly, was introduced by Mr Harry Pryce. As well as the cars – a Morris Traveller, Austin-Morris 1100, Morris Oxford, Humber and Ford Anglia – the whole scene has changed today, apart from Bricknell's building on the extreme right. The Congregational Chapel closed in the 1970s and was later demolished, as were the shops. (HP)

The band played for the opening of the Oxfam shop. By the end of the century there would be a plethora of charity shops in the town. The old buildings in the background would later make way for the Tesco store, while in the left foreground the driver of a Ford Corsair has claimed one of the last parking spaces in Duke Street, so convenient for shopping. (HP)

An aerial view of the town centre, dating from after the construction of the new town centre. (IM)

Moving west, one can make out St Austell's only high-rise development that was in keeping with the times, Park House flats at Bridge Road, of twelve storeys (and their shadow), dating the photograph to the late 1960s. (IM)

St Austell's 'new' cricket ground, 19 May 1956. In the background can be seen the Brewery and the houses in Trevarthian Road. On this site the Sixth Form College would later be built, opening in September 1974. (GE)

Trenance viaduct, showing the old pillars that the previous old wooden spider viaduct was built upon, photographed on 4 November 1956. (JW)

THE TOWN

St Austell railway station was far more atmospheric during the age of steam. Steam locomotive 7925, 'Westal Hall' from Paddington, heads out of the station towards Penzance at 1.30pm on 2 August 1956. (JW)

Another view of St Austell railway station. This time steam locomotive 5058, 'County of Colmorvan', is heading for Penzance on 1 June 1960. (JW)

The 1008 'Earl of Cloneaty' at St Austell station on 3 June 1960. It is interesting to note the telegraph poles and a multitude of cables running next to the track. The footbridge over the line remains today, although the station buildings have been replaced. (JW)

The interior of St Austell signal-box, showing a large diagram of the layout of the track. The signal-box is now abandoned. (RS)

Stephens and Pope Ltd.
St. Austell

Telephone Nos. 139 & 539

CORNWALL'S LEADING WHOLESALERS

We Keep You on the Right Lines

Grocery, Provisions, Tobacco, Confectionery, Chemist Sundries

* * * *

Come and have a cup of tea and a cake with us at STANDS 7 and 8. It's "Bud" Tea, too! Cakes with "RED RING" Flour, of course!

* * * *

Two Australian girls are anxious to tell you about their country and their products. We may have the Ashes but they have the Goods! We know—we SELL them.

* * * *

Catering Hygiene is vital to us all . . .
Use DEOSAN Products and be SAFE

* * * *

Stand Nos. 7 & 8

An advertisement for Stephens & Pope Ltd, 'Cornwall's leading wholesalers'. This was one of a number of advertisements for local firms that appeared in the *Cornish Guardian* on 10 March 1955 as they prepared for the St Austell Ideal Home and Trades Exhibition which ran for ten days at the Public Rooms. There were 24 exhibitors, 13 of them being based in the St Austell area.

Chapter Two
⟐ LOCAL BUSINESSES ⟑

Stephens & Pope Ltd's premises at Trenance during the 1950s. They had previously been based at Grant's Walk. Mainly operating as wholesale grocers, the firm covered an area including Fowey, Polruan, Mevagissey, Portloe, St Mawes, Truro, Falmouth, Padstow and Newquay, as well as various places en route. (AD)

Participants in Stephens & Pope Ltd's free staff trip to Plymouth in March 1953. Freeman's luxury coach took the men to watch Plymouth Argyle, while the ladies went shopping. Then they all met at a restaurant where they enjoyed a meal together.

In 1955 a flat-bed trailer ran away down Church Street and crashed through the shop front of Julian Pascoe in Vicarage Place. As can be seen, considerable damage was done to the shop, but fortunately no one was injured. (JS)

Woolworth's staff, spring 1958. The store had recently been refurbished, taking in the top part of Chandors Place as well as a former butcher's shop which housed the confectionery section. The *Cornish Guardian* reported on 27 March 1958: 'Shoppers can move about the store with more freedom and the new plastic-tile floor makes the whole place much quieter. The store, brilliantly lit with electric strip lighting, has been fitted with extra ventilators with four extractors fitted on to the flat roofs.' (MO)

LOCAL BUSINESSES

A stylised drawing of Morgan Brothers in an advertisement from the early 1960s.

A British Road Services lorry is seen in front of their workshops in the old chapel at St Blazey. It is taking tanks produced by Tourell to a new atomic power station being built near Manchester. The destination might have been closer if some people had got their way, as a report in the *Cornish Guardian* on 2 May 1957 stated: 'The building of an atomic energy station in the area as the solution to the unemployment problem in and around St Austell was put forward at a meeting of the St Austell and District Unemployment Committee... It was contended that industry might spring up around the cheap power of an atom plant as history had shown it to have done around the cheap power of coal mines.' A similar scheme at Luxulyan was mooted in the early 1980s. (AD)

ST AUSTELL – *The Golden Years*

British Road Services, running from Falmouth to Birkenhead, carrying a rather large ship's funnel. The lorries were based at London Apprentice. (AD)

The 'Lorry Driver of the Year Competition', some time in the early 1960s. The contestants are seen here at Par Docks with their respective vehicles. An Everard clay ship can be seen in the background. (AD)

LOCAL BUSINESSES

THE MOST MODERN GARAGE IN THE WEST COUNTRY

PHILLIPS & GEAKE LTD.

MAIN  DEALERS

SLADES ROAD. ST. AUSTELL

TELEPHONE 2333—4 LINES

The DIRECTORS cordially invite all their customers to the official opening of their NEW GARAGE AND SHOWROOM by K. H. Searle, Esq. (Home Sales Manager of Fords of Great Britain) on

MONDAY, NOVEMBER 4th, at 11.30 a.m.

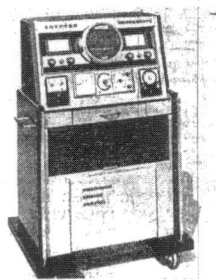

UNIQUE NEW VEHICLE DISPLAY

TO COMMEMORATE THIS OPENING WE INTEND TO STAGE ONE OF THE WEST COUNTRY'S GREATEST-EVER DISPLAYS OF FORD

CARS, VANS AND LORRIES

DEMONSTRATIONS (BY APPOINTMENT) ON MOST MODELS.

BODYWORK & PAINT SHOP

WE HAVE INSTALLED A SPECIAL BODY JIG FOR THE REPAIR OF CRASHED VEHICLES. ALL BODYWORK, REPAIRS AND PAINT-SPRAYING ARE OUR SPECIALITY!

SERVICE WHILE YOU WAIT!!

WITH OUR NEW EQUIPMENT WE CAN NOW GIVE SPEEDY NORMAL SERVICE & CAR WASHING ON ALL MAKES OF CARS, WHILE YOU HAVE COFFEE IN THE LOUNGE!

The Laycock Speed Car-Wash

GREAT LATE NEWS FLASH!!
WE ARE THE ONLY RETAILERS IN CORNWALL OF THE
FAMOUS CHEAPER
JET
PETROL
ON SALE FROM TODAY!!

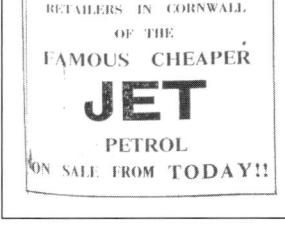

A section of the new Showroom.

FORD ON SHOW WEEK
(NOVEMBER 4th–9th)

- We cordially ask all our FORD customers who desire a free service inspection to telephone us at St. Austell 2333. Please hurry as bookings are heavy.
- MANY INTERESTING DISPLAY FEATURES AND WORKING CUTAWAY ENGINES
- REFRESHMENTS
- COMPETITIONS — PRIZES
- TEST YOUR SKILL ON THE BRAKE REACTION TESTER
- CORTINA LOTUS AND ANGLIA EAST AFRICAN SAFARI CLASS WINNER ON SHOW

In October 1963 Phillips & Geake Ltd boasted 'The most modern garage in the West Country.' This full-page advertisement appeared in the *Cornish Guardian* on 31 October 1963 to annouce the official opening of the company's new garage and showroom in Slades Road. A Ford main dealer, Ford Corsairs dominate the display, while a large floodlight is mounted on the wall in the foreground. The houses in Courtney Road can been seen above the petrol kiosk, but the view would be obscured later when Fairfield Park estate was created in the fields adjoining the garage, also appropriating the venue for the popular annual fair.

XMAS GREETINGS
from the
WHITE HART GARAGE
ST. AUSTELL
Your Appointed Nuffield Retail Dealers

Morris - Wolseley - Riley - M.G.

*MORRIS SIX SALOON
*MORRIS OXFORD SALOON
MORRIS OXFORD TRAVELLER'S CAR
MORRIS MINOR SALOON
MORRIS MINOR TRAVELLER'S CAR
MORRIS MINOR TOURER

WE HAVE THE SELECTION

*MORRIS COWLEY 10 cwt. VAN
*MORRIS COWLEY 10 cwt. PICK-UP
MORRIS MINOR 5 cwt. VAN
MORRIS MINOR 5 cwt. PICK-UP

WOLSELEY 6/80 SALOON
WOLSELEY 4/44 SALOON

YOU HAVE THE CHOICE

RILEY PATHFINDER
RILEY 1½ LITRE SALOON

M.G. MAGNETTE
M.G. T.F. SPORTS

EXCHANGES   DEMONSTRATIONS   DEFERRED TERMS
LITERATURE ON REQUEST

*Immediate Delivery

OTHER MODELS EARLY OR ROTATIONAL DELIVERY

Phone St. Austell 60

An advertisement for White Hart Garage, Easter Hill, St Austell, which appeared in the *Cornish Guardian* on 24 December 1953. An interesting range of cars and vans was on offer at the time, but only MG has survived.

LOCAL BUSINESSES

Hill & Phillips advertising the 1957-model Vauxhalls with 'extras' including a heater, windscreen washers and American-influenced whitewall tyres. The advert appeared in the *Cornish Guardian* on 23 August 1956.

A splendid aerial view of the John Williams' premises, with the cattle market, bypass and Pentewan roundabout in the foreground. The scene is dramatically different today. (CR)

John Williams' staff outside the Art Deco John Williams office building at Pentewan Road, visible in the bottom right of the previous picture, c.1970. The flags were flying to celebrate a royal visit. (MCPS)

LOCAL BUSINESSES

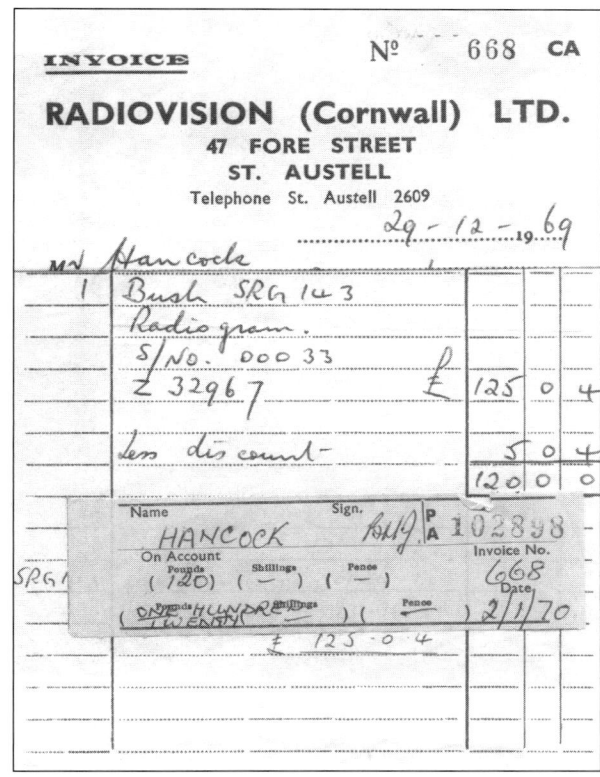

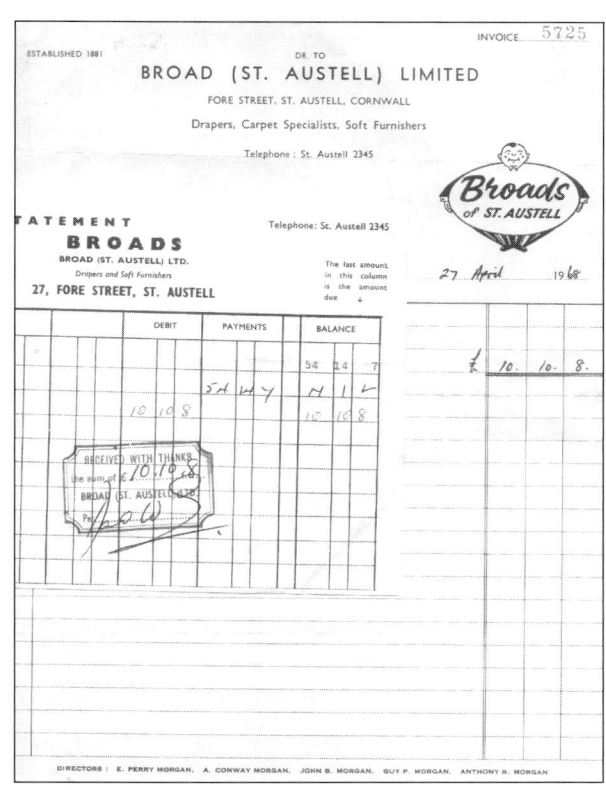

Above left: An invoice from Radiovision (Cornwall) Ltd who, at the time, had premises in Fore Street. A new Bush radiogram could be purchased for £125.

Above right: A sales invoice and statement from Broad (St Austell) Ltd, April 1968.

Left: A receipt from St Austell Furnishing Co. from May 1961 for a new carpet. By now they had acquired the Public Rooms. The last music festival to be held there was on 6 December 1956.

LOCAL BUSINESSES

Above left: The 'Fashbar', a trendy 1960s boutique, was part of Sydney Grose Ltd, as advertised in the *Cornish Guardian* on 22 August 1963.

Above right: *The Dam Busters*, showing wartime exploits that had occurred only a short period earlier, was screened at the Capitol Theatre from 8 August 1955. This advertisement appeared in the *Cornish Guardian* on 4 August 1955.

Left: For many years W.H. Smith occupied the corner shop at 1 Fore Street, opposite the church. This lovely period advertisement featuring a Diana Rigg look-alike is from the *Cornish Guardian* of 27 April 1967.

A poster for St Austell Week, 22–27 August 1966. Events included a bathing-beauty competition and women's football, with Westward TV participating. A baby show and 'Old Tyme Music Hall' helped provide something for everyone. (HP)

Chapter Three
◖ AROUND THE COAST ◗

Franked in August 1950, this postcard shows Mevagissey's outer harbour looking across The Pool towards Polkirt Hill. At first glance this view appears to be little changed today, however, the Harbour Lights public house at the top of Polkirt Hill has been replaced by a large apartment block, and fish stores have been built under the facing cliff. Interestingly, the base of the unusual lamp on the right still stands next to the footpath. The area in the foreground was known locally as 'The Battery'. Beyond it, the 'Nest' of the Watchhouse rises above the roof of the museum.

During a storm on the night of 18/19 February 1968 the harbour wall at Mevagissey was breached and the Sea Gull Café destroyed. The roof and wall of the neighbouring boat yard of W. Frazier & Son was also damaged. The café was never rebuilt. (MMu)

An aerial view of Mevagissey. The postcard was franked in July 1952, but the actual photograph can be dated to about 1948.

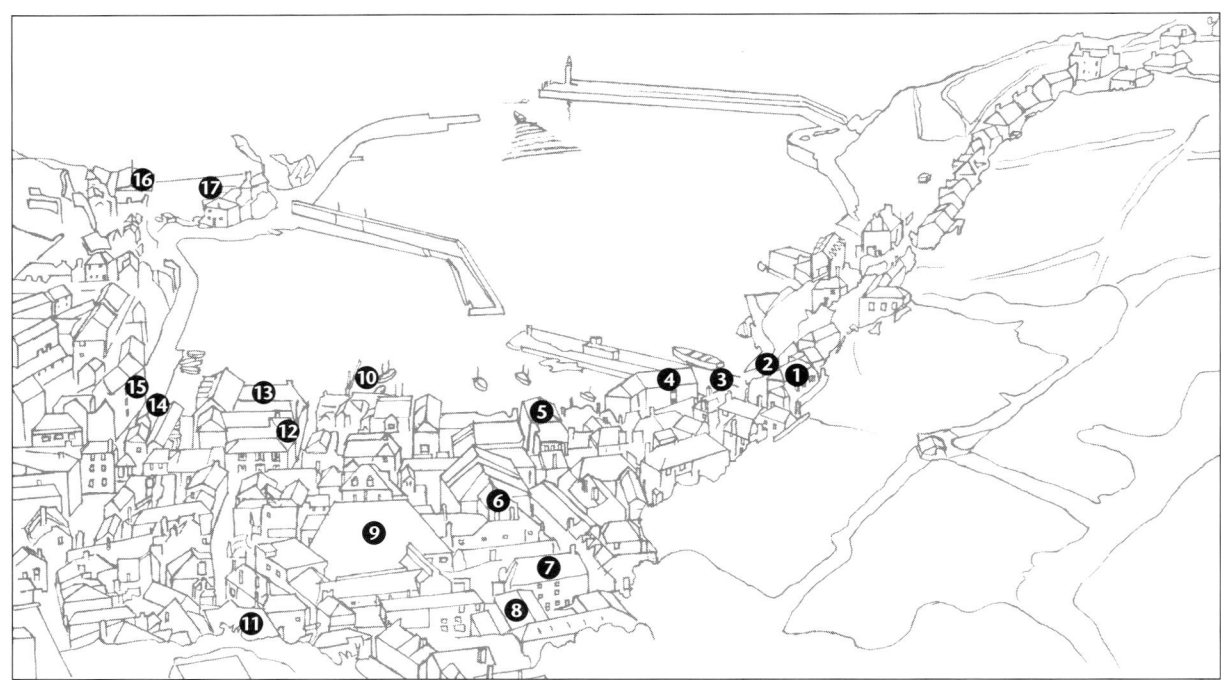

A period of change for Mevagissey.

AROUND THE COAST

Key to drawing:

1 Lily Court situated on Polkirt Hill. The cottages there were old and in a very bad state of repair but, nevertheless, continued to be occupied until the late 1950s. When they were eventually demolished garages were built on the site.

2 There were two blacksmith's shops in Mevagissey – this one on Polkirt Hill, and the other in Chapel Street. This area behind Church Street, to the left of the photograph, was known locally as 'The Backlet'. Both these properties have since been converted into living accommodation.

3 & 12 There were two coal merchants in Mevagissey – one on the West Quay used by W. Prynn & Son, and the other off Jetty Street run by Farran Brothers. Both have long since ceased trading, with the premises renovated into living accommodation.

4 These buildings are situated on the west side of the harbour. During the 1950s they were used as fishermen's lofts, where fishing nets, lines and various items of equipment were stored. Eventually the ground floor was converted into shops and the floors above into living accommodation.

5, 10, 13 & 15 These were stores, all connected with fishing, and were occupied by three local fish buyers, Messrs Pawlyn, Robins and Edwards. Fishing flourished, particularly during the 1950s, and Mevagissey became an extremely busy fishing port.

6 & 7 At the foot of Polkirt Hill, in the year 1842, a Wesleyan Chapel was built. For many years regular services were held here, until the building was considered to have become unsafe and was finally demolished in 1970, together with all the old cottages (7) in the immediate vicinity known as 'The Meadow'. Flats have since been built on the site and are known as Wesley Court.

8 To the rear of Wesley Court there were stores, also connected with the fishing industry, but now the well-known and popular Mevagissey Model Railway occupy the ground floor and there are flats on the floor above.

9 A Fish Factory was built at the foot of Tregoney Hill where Pawlyn Bros Fish Merchants of Mevagissey continued in business for many years. In the 1950s the factory was taken over by a firm called Newball & Mason, and canning fish continued until the fishing industry declined. Many years later the premises were demolished and flats built on the site – known in 2004 as Rebecca's Court.

11 Here, on Tregoney Hill, another little chapel had been built. After being closed for many years it was re-opened and, for a short while, was used as a carpenter's shop. Ultimately, however, the building was completely demolished.

14 For many years these premises were used as a marine engineering workshop, but latterly were converted into several small shops.

16 On the east side of the harbour the long-established boat yard was owned by W. Frazier & Son who were kept very busy after the war years, when fishing boats and pleasure craft were in great demand. They also catered for the maintenance of the local fishing fleet that had sadly been neglected during the war years when materials were very scarce. The business continued until 1977 when the proprietors retired.

17 Included in the property of W. Frazier & Son was another yard in which huts were erected for the convenience of the Mevagissey Swimming Club. These remained until the club was finally disbanded in the 1950s. Adjoining this yard is a building which was erected in 1742. In the 1950s the ground floor was used for storing boats and equipment during the winter, while the first floor was used as fishermen's lofts. After much renovation the property, which was then renamed Frazier House, became the home of Mevagissey Museum, and is very successfully managed by the Mevagissey and District Museum Society. This venture has proved to be a very popular attraction with locals and visitors alike.

W. Frazier & Son's boat yard and the Sea Gull Café, Mevagissey, in 1961. (WAF)

Left: *The Queen of the Fal* passenger vessel being launched from W. Frazier & Son's yard in 1953. The Sea Gull Café can be seen in the background. The boat still exists, although now renamed the *Cornish Belle*, and operates from Tolverne on the Fal. (MMu)

Below: Two Mevagissey fishermen, 'Alf' and 'Piper' Dunn, heaving a conger on board their boat in 1959. (MMu)

Brothers Caleb and James Furse caught bringing conger and ling ashore at Mevagissey in 1959. Their boat was *The Little Pearl*. (MMu)

A fine catch! Sadly, most of this large pilchard haul on 13 August 1965, seen on board the *Lindy Lou*, was thrown overboard because of a lack of canning facilities in the port at the time. A canning factory for pilchards and sardines had been established in the 1880s and operated until 1965. Jeff Blamey is seen looking ashore, while Edgar 'Egger' Hocking is busy behind him. The boys are Tommy and Peter Blamey and Michael Claydon. (MMu)

Eddie Lakeman and his son Andrew, landing a shark at Mevagissey, c.1970. (MMu)

An unfortunate accident – and something that would become a theme with lorries during the 'Golden Years'. Prynn's coal lorry backed into Mevagissey Harbour during 1950. Prynn's store can be seen in the background, along with the petrol pumps that stood there until fairly recently. (MMu)

The yacht *Petit Brettone* being launched at Portmellon in 1960. It was built by G.P. Mitchell & Son of Portmellon. (MMu)

Mevagissey Town Hall in Church Street. It was demolished during the 1960s, an unpopular move with many locals who hold fond memories of events held in the building. (MMu)

AROUND THE COAST

A postcard illustrating the attractions of St Austell Bay. Noteworthy aspects of the pictures are the clay ship *Lady Sophia* entering Charlestown's inner harbour past the old vertically-hinged lock gates, and the plethora of beach huts immediately behind Par Beach.

A lovely view looking across St Austell Bay towards Black Head from the fields above Charlestown. Today the mine tips at the end of the field are hidden by a small copse of trees, but otherwise the vista has not changed.

An aerial view of Porthpean, before the sea wall was built behind the beach, or the golf course occupied the fields in the background. The Hideaway public house in the middle left above the cliffs has since been turned into a private residence.

Another view of Porthpean Beach, little changed today apart from the sea wall behind the beach.

The construction of a new vestry at the south-eastern corner of Charlestown Church was marked by a stone-laying ceremony on 20 October 1963. The vicar at the time was R.E. Beer. The steeple – of fibreglass – would not be added until 1971. (GE)

Carlyon Bay Hotel seen in splendid isolation. It would not be like this for much longer.

A postcard from Duporth Holiday Park, showing Charles Rashleigh's former home, demolished in 1988, as well as the beach and chalets.

AROUND THE COAST

There was a big fire at Duporth Holiday Park in early June 1961. The gutted remains of the dining-rooms and dance hall can be seen here, and dozens of chalets were also destroyed. (GE)

The beach at Carlyon Bay with its familiar stack. The beach huts, the Cornish Riviera Lido Club, and the tennis-courts are but memories. Badminton, squash and swimming were also popular pastimes here.

The Cornish Riviera Lido Club boasted a fine outdoor swimming-pool, the largest in the Westcountry, which was used by residents and visitors alike. Local schools without their own pools used it for swimming lessons. The author recalls arriving in a new coach equipped with wooden bench seats (no seat belts back then), before attempting to swim across the shallow end in the foreground. (HP)

The ballroom. Dinner dances, Olde Tyme Music Hall, receptions and comedy shows made it a popular venue. Meanwhile, the hall, with a capacity of more than 2,000 people, was used for concerts, international wrestling events and bathing-beauty contests. (HP)

AROUND THE COAST

By the end of the era the tennis-courts had given way to car parking. Soon the beach huts, café, paddling pool and pavilion would also be gone.

A steam train passing Par Beach on its journey from Fowey on 10 July 1957. The tennis-courts on the right are still in use. (JW)

A view of Spit Cottages, Par, before their demolition in about 1968, with the harbour and clay ships dominating the scene. (WhM)

Another view of Spit Cottages, as well as the Cornwall Mills building behind. (WhM)

Viewed from the beach, Spit Cottages were clearly in the way of an ever-expanding harbour catering for the export of china clay. (IM)

Chapter Four
❦ CHANGING SCHOOLS ❧

Penrice School, Charlestown Road, opened on 11 January 1960. There was some debate about the choice of site prior to the school's construction, with some favouring Rocky Park. However, it was felt that the western edge of the town should not be developed, thus ensuring that St Mewan was not absorbed into the town. (GE)

The opening of Penrice School. A view of the first assembly, 11 January 1960. (GE)

Carclaze Infant School concert, held at Carclaze Chapel, c.1968.

Carclaze Infant School pupils with their teacher, Mrs Hawkey, on the grass in front of Carclaze Chapel, c.1968.

CHANGING SCHOOLS

The Lawn School, St Austell, 1950/51. The children are pictured with their teacher, Mrs Kellow. The school was founded in 1901 and closed during the 1970s. The ethos of the school was reflected in its motto, 'If you would reach the mark, aim high.' (MB)

The Lawn School's gymnasium, complete with wall bars, benches and a rope ladder. Pictures of various movements are displayed on the end wall. (BS)

Blantyre. The new centre for the training of adult mentally-handicapped people was photographed by George Ellis for the local papers upon its completion on 21 October 1963.

Form 1a, Mount Charles Junior School, July 1965. Class sizes of 37 are still, unfortunately, common today. (MG)

CHANGING SCHOOLS

A new swimming-pool, ideal for young learners, being opened at Mount Charles School on 30 May 1964. It was officially opened by Miss Williams, former headmistress. The old Silvanus Trevail-designed school, since turned into apartments, can be seen in the background. (GE)

After making a five-day tour of Belgium in June 1968, along with their headmaster, Mr H. A. Williams and six teachers, 70 pupils from Mount Charles Junior School are seen disembarking from their coaches outside the school. As well as visiting Ostend, Bruges and Brussels, they also stopped off in London where they saw the Changing of the Guard and were fortunate to see the Queen as she emerged for the Horse Guards' Parade. (CGU)

In 1966 the Prime Minister, Harold Wilson, opened nine new schools in Cornwall. He is seen here on 29 October 1966 declaring open the new school at Biscovey. (GE)

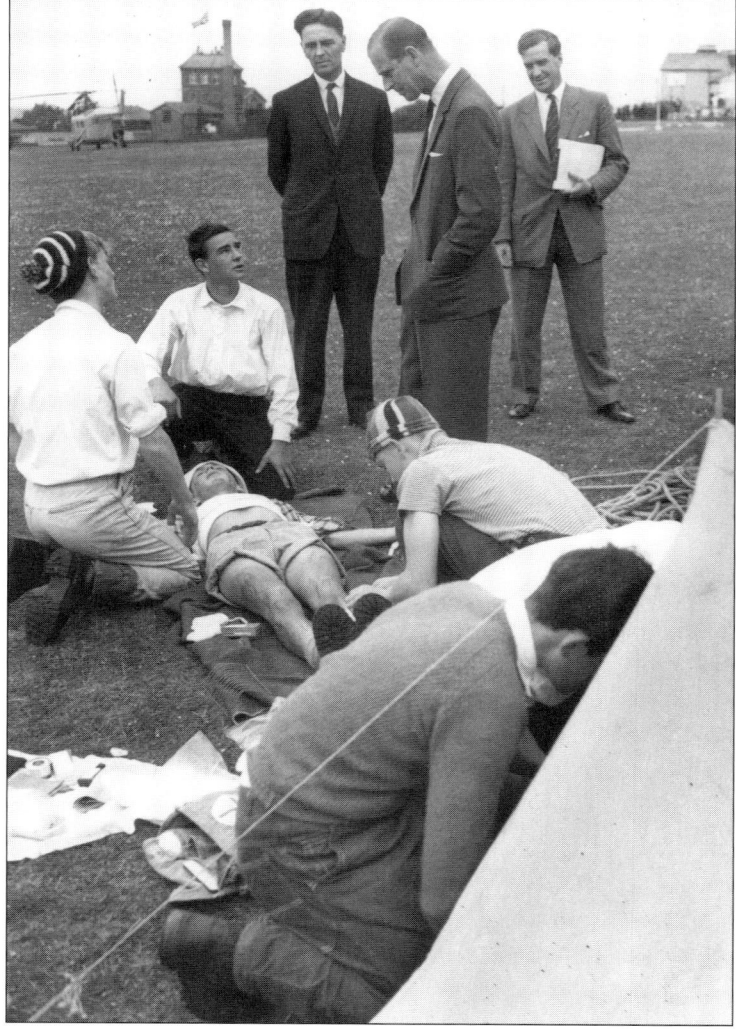

The Duke of Edinburgh visited St Austell Grammar School for Boys on 6 May 1961, arriving by helicopter which landed on the school playing-field. He is pictured talking to two Newquay boys. Various displays were given representing dinghy sailing, model-making, camping and trampolining, and E.C.L.P. apprentices demonstrated judo. The Brewery tower can be seen in the background. Other stops on the Duke's itinerary included a tour of the china-clay works. (GE)

Chapter Five
AT WORK

Left: The new china-clay silo at Burngullow photographed during construction on 11 February 1958. Much larger ones were subsequently built nearby and remain a prominent feature in 2004. (WhM)

Below: Building work in progress at E.C.L.P.'s new headquarters, John Keay House, on 10 March 1965. Construction had begun in September 1963 to provide the company with new office space with a total floor area of 81,000 square feet that would be able to accommodate 450 staff. A Ford Anglia van can be seen on the unmade road. (WhM)

An aerial view of Par Harbour. The port was busy throughout the 1950s and '60s, requiring enlargements and improvements to be made. Some 800 shipping movements a year were taking place by 1956. (A Court Photographs Ltd, c/o WHM)

It wasn't all hard work! An atmospheric shot of Par Harbour showing the Everard vessel *Clarity* – many of their ships' names ended in 'ity'. A steam-operated crane can be seen on the right. (IM)

AT WORK

Loading bagged clay at Par Harbour. Spit Cottages can be seen behind the Ruston Bucyrus 22-RB crane. On the right is a conveyor used for the bulk loading of china clay. (IM)

A Heavy Transport lorry discharging china clay on to a ship at Par, via a conveyor and shute. The lorry is painted in the familiar light blue and white livery. Road transport became more important to the clay companies as the 1950s progressed. (WHM)

ST AUSTELL – *The Golden Years*

The steam locomotive 'Judy' at Par Harbour. The squat design was to allow the engine to pass under the low bridge below the main Paddington to Penzance line. It was constructed in 1937 by W.G. Bagnall Ltd of Stafford. (WHM)

'Judy', unnamed at the time, at Par Harbour on 7 August 1956. (JW)

'Alfred', purchased in 1953, followed by 'Judy'. The engines were the inspiration for Revd W. Audry's Bill and Ben in the 'Thomas the Tank Engine' books, as well as being popular with children on school trips to the port. They were used at Par until 1977, and are now in the custody of Bodmin and Wenford Railway. (WHM)

AT WORK

The railway line to Fowey. This photograph was taken just before the track was ripped up and the route developed as a road by E.C.C. A diesel locomotive and clay wagons are seen pulling into Fowey station. The railway closed at the beginning of January 1965. (WhM)

The Par end of St Pinnock Tunnel on the Fowey branch line, photographed on 5 May 1957. The sign to the right of the tunnel mouth says 'All down goods and mineral trains must stop dead here.' (JW)

The transformation of the railway between Par and Fowey into a road, with Fowey station in the background, 1968. (WhM)

A view across Par Harbour showing Cornwall Mills Ltd, who ground china stone for the production of abrasive cleaners and porcelain. In the middle distance a ship is being loaded amidst clouds of dust. E.C.L.P. acquired Cornwall Mills in September 1955. (IM)

AT WORK

Open spaces at Par Harbour were used for sawmills, storing pipes and other paraphernalia. Since then new refining tanks and dries have been built here. April 1957 marked the end of an era, as the Tregaskes family stopped shipbuilding at Par. (IM)

More construction work at Par Harbour, photographed on 3 September 1970. Here new driers and linhays, or clay stores, are being built. (IM)

Above left: Wet clay could be a hazard at Par Docks. Here a lorry trailer has slipped off the dockside and onto a boat. (AD)

Above right: A similar mishap at Par Docks involving a 1962 Ford Trader. (AD)

Left: After the war old military equipment was often found to be useful. Here an ex-Army trailer is seen waiting to be tipped at Par Harbour some time during the 1950s. (AD)

A giant bulldozer, a Michigan 280, helps load an earth scraper with sand. (IM)

AT WORK

Washing clay from the pit face with a high-pressure hose or monitor. These operate at up to 300psi (20bar) and systematically rake the rock to remove the clay. (IM)

The interior of Goverseth refining plant. With production methods improving and sales buoyant, on 26 July 1966 E.C.L.P. received the Queen's Award for Industry. (IM)

The control room at Goverseth refining plant, showing what was state-of-the-art equipment at the time. The first computer to be used for production-related work was introduced at Treviscoe in 1967. (IM)

The second rotary drying kiln to be installed, in 1947. (IM)

AT WORK

One of the jobs to be undertaken in the clay companies' laboratories was to carry out a particle-size determination test... (IM)

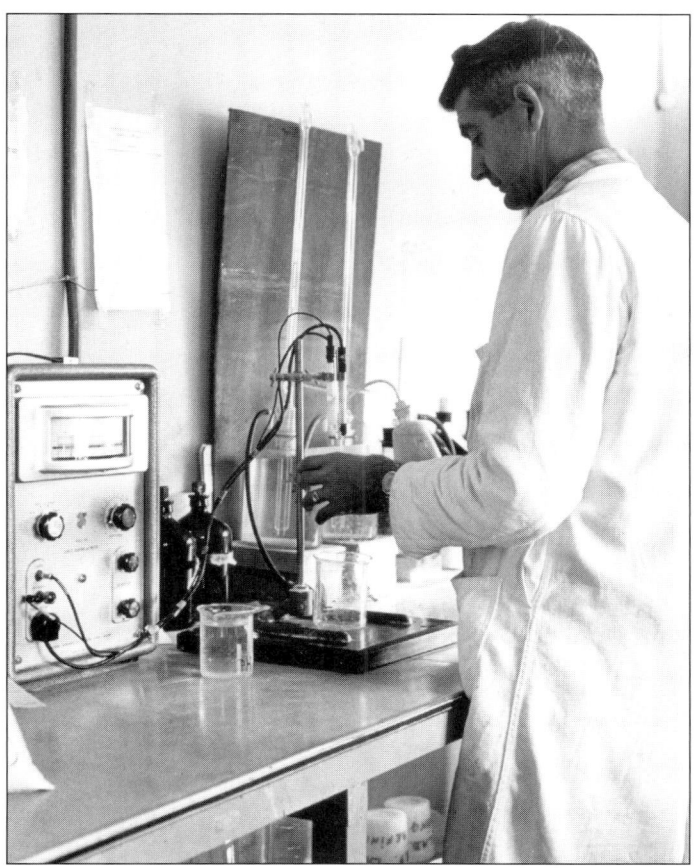

...as well as conducting a pH test of samples. (IM)

Loading bulk clay into an ocean-going vessel at Fowey was a dusty process. (IM)

It is 1952, and the last set of shaft pumps to be installed in the St Austell area is recorded at Bodelva china-clay pit. Of course, this is now the location of the Eden Project. (WHM)

AT WORK

St Austell Fire Brigade in 1957. They were based at St Austell Fire Station in Bodmin Road. This had been built in 1939 and served the local community until it was replaced with a state-of-the-art facility at Polkyth in 2003. (CCFB)

St Austell Fire Brigade, 1960. Major incidents dealt with by the town's fire brigade included a blaze at Carlyon Bay Hotel on 27 December 1931, and when a major fire occurred at the Co-op store in the town on 18 October 1940. (CCFB)

Above: Pannier-tank engines 1627 and 8713 outside St Blazey engine sheds, and in front of the engine turntable on 5 September 1959. Although little evidence of the track remains, in 2004 the fine buildings are still used for light industry. (JW)

Right: Bugle signal-box. Signalman P.O. Roberts is at the window in April 1965. The Par to Newquay branch line, so important to the tourist industry, was spared Dr Beeching's 'axe' in 1967. (JW)

Below: Steam locomotive 3635 outside St Blazey engine sheds on 5 May 1957. (JW)

Chapter Six
SPORT

In 1949 a new speedway track was opened on a 14-acre site at Par Moor, providing more up-to-date facilities than those at Rocky Park that had been used since 1930. The inaugural meeting at the 360-yard track took place on Tuesday 14 June when some 12,000 people attended. The local team was soon known as the Gulls and they are seen here in the early 1950s. Left to right, back row: Ray Ellis, Maurice Mattingly, John Yates, Norman Street, Harold Bull, Jack Luke; front row: Ken James, ?, Billy Sobey. (RB)

One of the great names in speedway at this time was the England international, Jack Parker. He not only provided assistance in the design of the Cornish Stadium, but also officially switched on the new floodlights in August 1949 – as well as establishing a new track record whilst there. (RB)

Other visiting riders included Jack Biggs. He captained the Australian Kangaroos team when they raced against the English Lions at the Cornish Stadium on 20 October 1949. The home side won 44–39. (RB)

Local riders included the captain, Norman Street, and Harold Bull. They were supported by Allan Quinn (an Aussie), Max Rech (a Polish rider) and the James brothers, 'Ticker' and Ken, from Poole. The Americans' top rider was Ernie Roccio.

The programme for the races involving the Cornish Gulls versus the American touring team in the 'Grand Challenge Match'. The result was an honourable draw with each team scoring 42 points. (IT)

SPORT

The American touring team visited the Cornish Stadium to take on the local Gulls on 21 August 1951. (GE)

Speedway action – Cornish Gulls v. Swindon – 6 May 1952. (GE)

At the speedway meeting held on 16 September 1952 the helicopter was brought in to entertain the crowds with a demonstration flight to celebrate Battle of Britain Week. It was supposed to carry out a night landing in the centre of the track using its own searchlight. However, as it descended, at about 50 feet from the ground it veered sideways. It crashed through the boundary fence, ending up on top of three coaches. Tragically, the co-pilot and a spectator, Mr James Richards of Penryn, were killed, while three other spectators were seriously injured. The accident was attributed to a mechanical fault in the engine. (IT)

SPORT

A close-up of the crash. The mangled remains of the helicopter lying on its side are being inspected by service personnel. The rotor blades sliced open the roofs of the coaches and brought down the boundary fencing. (DS)

The damaged coaches are seen here with the crashed helicopter behind them. The middle vehicle, JAF826, belonged to Westbourne Motors of St Austell, while the right-hand one, LRL660, was run by Willis of Bodmin. The devastation shows that the accident could have been much worse, had the helicopter landed in the crowds. (DS)

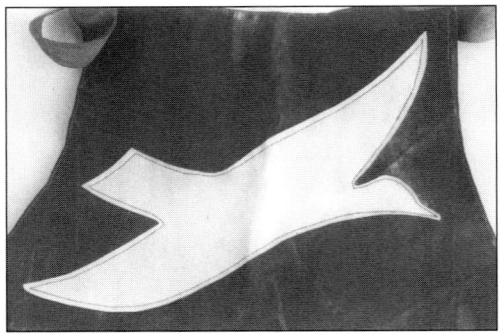

Above: A tabbard, as worn by the Gulls, showing the white seagull on a royal-blue background. (IT)

Left: A 'Lucky Programme' for St Austell Gulls v. Plymouth Devils on 7 August 1962. (IT)

Right: A similar programme for the qualifying round of the Provincial Riders' Championship. Solo speedway events ceased at the Cornish Stadium at the end of the 1963 season. Side-cars continued, but by now priority was given to stock-car and banger racing. The site was sold in 1986 to create Stadium Retail Park – for many locals a sad end to a memorable venue. (IT)

Below: A St Austell Speedway Supporters' Club badge, dating from 1952. The enamel lapel badge shows the seagull motif along with a red Cornish pixie. (IT)

SPORT

On 26 April 1954 Sir Stanley Matthews came to St Austell to play in a football match. He is seen here chatting to Ray Boundy and Roy Rivers (Camelford) before the game. Mr Boundy recalls him saying, 'I'm playing for Old England in a few days and we want to turn out and teach Young England a thing or two' – in other words, not to be too aggressive! (RBo)

Stanley Matthews in action at St Austell, playing in the position of outside right. St Austell County School can be seen in the background. Matthews had previously visited the town in 1949. (RBo)

ST AUSTELL – *The Golden Years*

Another shot of the same match. It can been seen that it was well attended, with a crowd estimated at 10,000 people. (RBo)

St Austell A.F.C. Pictured are, left to right: Maurice Babb, Billy Way, Dicky Hendicott, Freddie York, Dave Northcott, Brian Powell, Dave Lean, Mike Aitken, Derek Baxter, Brian Rimes, Maurice Opie (First Aid), Ray Brett. They had removed their boots because the ground was so hard that their feet hurt! (RB)

SPORT

The souvenir programme for the match in which Stanley Matthews played as the guest captain. It was printed by the long-established local firm of H.E. Warne Ltd. (RBo)

ST AUSTELL – *The Golden Years*

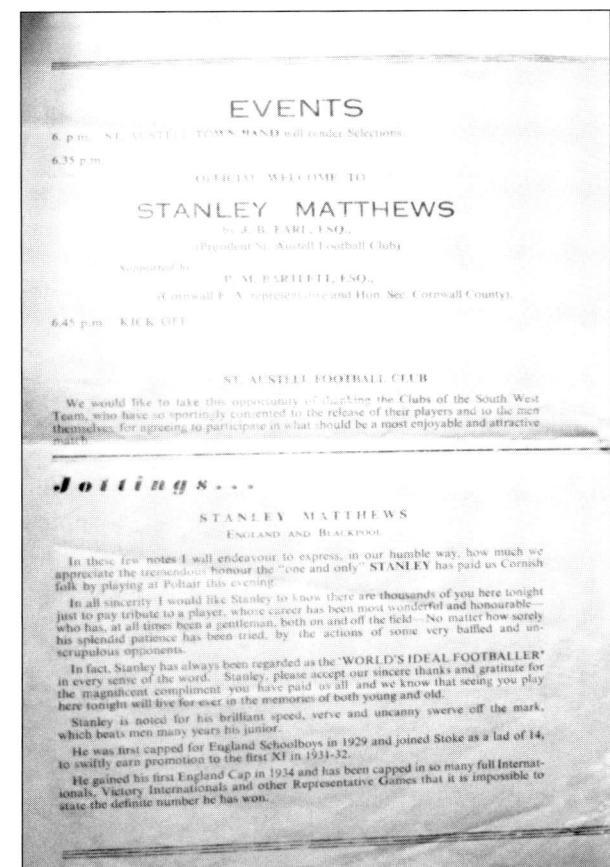

An evening to remember with the 'World's Ideal Footballer'. When St Austell played Carshalton Athletic on 4 February 1956 Stanley Matthews sent a 'good wishes' telegram before the game. That evening the crowd of some 5,000 people witnessed a 2–1 victory by the local side. (RBo)

The programme cover for the Cornwall v. Herefordshire match which took place in the afternoon of 6 March 1954 at St Austell. The official programme sold for the princely sum of 3d. (RBo)

SPORT

The final match of the season – as early as the end of April in 1954 – was between St Austell (augmented by South Western League guest stars) and the First Division team, Cardiff City. (RBo)

ST AUSTELL – *The Golden Years*

St Austell's 'Lilywhites' became the South Western League Champions in 1969. They also won the Senior Cup and Charity Cup that year, and were in the final of the S.W. League Cup. Unfortunately they lost to Tavistock (however, the following week they soundly beat them 9–1!). The players were, left to right, back row: Brian Morgan, Brian Powell, Maurice Babb, Freddie York, Brian Rimes, John Elliot; front row: Dave Northcott, Mike Aitken, Dave Lean, Derek Baxter, Ray Brett, Billy Way. Proudly displaying their trophies, the team are seen here with the committee at St Austell Rifle and Pistol Club. (RB)

A St Austell A.F.C. blazer badge, showing a football beneath the town's 'ragged cross' emblem.

SPORT

The Cornish Mines football team. The owner of the company, Mr John Yelland Hooper, bought the new strips for the team following their victory over Harveys of Falmouth. Mr Hooper was also the founder of the Cornish Riviera Club at Carlyon Bay. (HP)

The Y.M.C.A. football team, photographed in September 1968 at Par running track. Many of the players went on to play for the South Western League. (AD)

In the 1954/55 season Foxhole won the Junior Cup, the St Austell and District League Cup, and the Bodmin and District Cup. (RB)

SPORT

Foxhole Stars, 1955–56. The team are seen here at Bodmin after winning the Shipwrights' Cup. (RB)

ST. AUSTELL & DISTRICT FOOTBALL LEAGUE

SATURDAY, APRIL 19th. 1958
First Kick-off 2.45 p.m.

Official Programme

FINALS AT ST. AUSTELL

FINALISTS

FOXHOLE

v.

GERRANS

RUNNERS—UP

LERRYN

v.

TREGONY

Price - Threepence

The official programme for the final between Foxhole and Gerrans, played at St Austell on 19 April 1958. (RB)

Chapter Seven
❦ HAPPY DAYS ❧

St Austell Hospital carnival float during the 1950s, clearly showing that the staff were ready for any eventuality. (GG)

A Coronation Day arch was created outside the Duke of Cornwall public house at Mount Charles on 2 June 1953. (GE)

Coronation Day, 2 June 1953. St Austell's Fore Street was decorated with bunting to celebrate the occasion. (GE)

HAPPY DAYS

Stenalees Coronation celebrations. The Carnival Queen presents an orderly queue of youngsters with their commemorative coronation mugs on 2 June 1953. (GE)

St Austell children enjoying a folk-dancing event at the Mount Charles recreation-ground on 25 June 1953. It is interesting to note the old bandstand in the background, where the new Mount Charles School now stands. (GE)

HAPPY DAYS

Heavy Transport's first children's Christmas party, held in Zion School Room, 1957. (AD)

By 1960 St Austell Church Hall had become the venue for Heavy Transport's Christmas party. Attentive children, filling half of the hall, are enjoying the entertainment. (AD)

St Austell Shopping Week was officially opened by Miss Commerce 1954, Sally May, outside the Market House on 8 October 1954. She is seen here walking through Fore Street with Derek Roy, just after the formal opening. (GE)

HAPPY DAYS

The winning float of the 1962 St Austell Carnival was by Cornish Mines Supplies displaying 'A Model Kitchen'. It is seen here parked just along the road from the Cornish Mines building on the left, and West Hill School, familiar to many in the town, is on the right. The view is very different today. (HP)

Bugle Band Contest, 15 June 1962. Mr T.J. Powell, the adjudicator, is seen conducting *Solomn Melody*. The West of England Bandsmen's Festival was started in 1912. It was held annually at Peniel on the outskirts of Bugle until 1967 when the venue changed to the football ground at Molinnis Park. (GE)

Even Dr Who's great adversaries, the daleks, joined in St Austell Carnival on 28 August 1965. They are seen here advancing along Fore Street. (GE)

Mr Harry Pryce, master of ceremonies at the Cornish Riviera Lido Club, announces the winner of Miss South Coast, 1967. (HP)

Mr Harry Pryce entertaining a group of children at the Cornish Riviera Club. He recalls they were singing *We All Live in a Yellow Submarine*, a popular anthem at the time after The Beatles reached number one in the charts in September 1966 with their double-A-sided single *Yellow Submarine* and *Eleanor Rigby*, keeping the Beach Boys' *God Only Knows* at number two. (HP)

The cast of St Austell Amateur Operatic Society's production of *Carousel* in March 1968. Billy Bigelow was played by Ivor Jago, Mrs Mullin by Patricia Beard, and Jill Medlin appeared as Julie Jordan. At the time the chairman of the society was Mr R.E. Sanders. (MCPS)

HAPPY DAYS

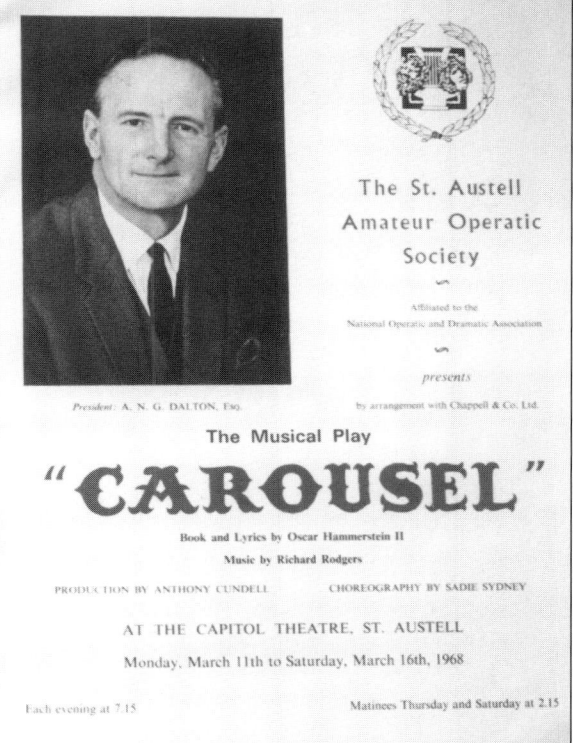

The programme for *Carousel*, showing the then president of St Austell Amateur Operatic Society, Mr A.N.G. Dalton, who was also managing director of E.C.L.P. at the time. (MG)

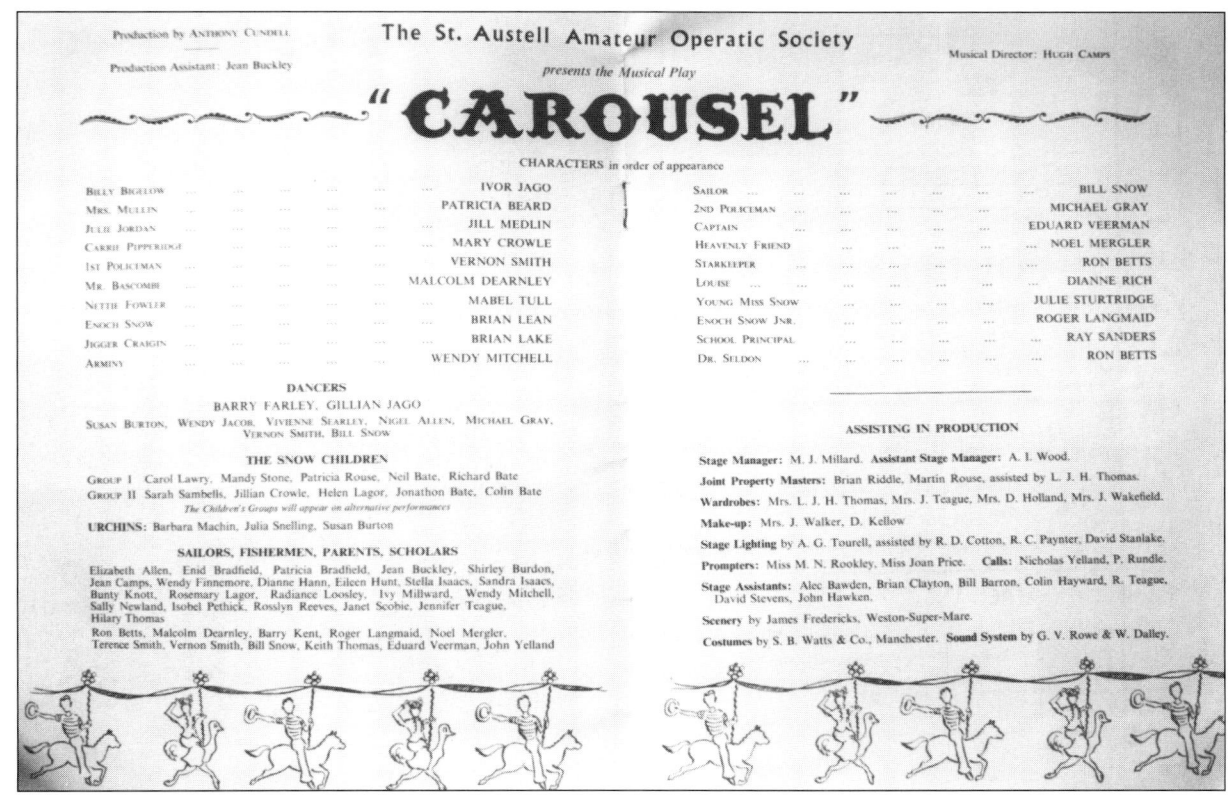

The cast of *Carousel*.

Other advertisements from local firms sponsoring the *Carousel* programme included estate agents S.A. Wilson and builders J.J. Jones & Son based in Courtney Road.

HAPPY DAYS

Local pop groups of the period included The Renegades, who were formed in 1959. The line-up was, left to right: Clive Letcher, Frank Trevains, Tony Langson, Brian Lawty and Brendon Joyce. (TL)

In about 1964, what would become a very popular local band, The Cousin Jacks, was formed. Seen here in a publicity photograph, the line-up was, left to right: Glen Rees, Michael Hooper, Tony Langson, Stephen Tucker and Paul Blackburn. (TL)

ST AUSTELL – *The Golden Years*

In 1964 The Cousin Jacks played at the Cavern Club in Liverpool the day after The Beatles, then continued their tour in Manchester and London, before returning to Menheniot (!) and The Bali Club in St Austell. This was St Austell's first ever disco, located upstairs from the Y.M.C.A. in Victoria Place. At one time they also played each week at the Cornish Riviera Club, Carlyon Bay, alongside some top names including The Kinks, The Pretty Things, The Troggs, Screaming Lord Sutch and Dave Dee, Dozy, Beaky, Mick and Tich. The resident trio was led by George (Drums) Mitchell. (TL)

HAPPY DAYS

Every self-respecting group of the time had to have their own van. The Cousin Jacks pose on the roof of their poster-adorned Commer van, which was a familiar sight around the town. They are, left to right: Glen Rees, Stuart Northcott, David Tucker, Tony Langson and Paul Blackburn (TL)

The Cousin Jacks, photographed at St Austell's multi-storey car park next to the town centre. Other popular local bands included Soul Society, featuring Spike Hooper, Beaver and The Saxons. (TL)

A series of trade fairs used to be held in the town centre and at the Cornish Riviera, Carlyon Bay. One such event was 'State 69'. (HP)

STATE 69

ST. AUSTELL and DISTRICT CHAMBER of COMMERCE

present their third

TRADES EXHIBITION

IN THE

NEW TOWN CENTRE

OCTOBER 7th to 11th

To be opened by

Stuart Hutchinson

(Westward Television)

at 12 noon, TUESDAY, OCTOBER 7th
Open daily from 2 p.m. to 9 p.m.
Admission 2/6 including Catalogue

Chamber of Commerce Officials:
President: E. H. H. Dorman, Esq.   Chairman: E. T. Higton, Esq.
Secretary: G. O. Ellis, Esq., Brookdale, Trevarrick, St. Austell
Treasurer: R. Sidey, Esq., Barclays Bank, Ltd., St. Austell

EXHIBITORS

Stand No.	Name
1	Warmawall (Bodmin) Ltd.
2	Bayly Bartlett Ltd.
3	County Typewriters—Office Equipment Co. Ltd.
4	Heltor (Cornwall) Ltd.
5	Barlows
6	Taylor and Low (Cornwall) Ltd.
7	Scott Brown Ltd.
8	C. Bricknell and Son
9	R. G. Clemo, The Poultry Shop, Ltd.
10	Zimber and Collins
11	Cornwall Electric Heat Ltd.
12	Parc Signs
14	Broads of St. Austell and Morgan Bros.
15	Western Insurance Brokers
15A	Frances Evans
16	A. and J. H. Phillips
17	British Red Cross Society, St. Austell Detach
18	South Western Gas Board
19	John E. Hickling
20	David Cock and Son
21	Margots
22	Greetings Cards (St. Austell) Ltd.
23	Fabwear Bazaar
25	English Clays Lovering Pochin Ltd.
26	R. and C. Daniell
27	Cornish Mines Supplies
28	G.P.O.
29	Royal National Lifeboat Institution
30	Pet and Garden Stores
31	Spastics Society, St. Austell Branch
32	Bobell Signs and Plastics
33	Gay Gowns
34	Anglian Double Glazing (Plymouth) Ltd.
35	C. and F. Watts Ltd.
36	Coal Utilisation Council
37	Hugo Veerman and Co.
38	Bray and Sons (Helston and St. Austell) Ltd.
39	Dayne Designs
40	Baha'i Faith
41	St. Peter's Church, Treverbyn
42	Colourvogue (H. J. and V. Stone)
	Clifden Restaurant, *Refreshment Bars*

A list of exhibitors at 'State 69'. Sadly many of the local firms no longer exist. (HP)

Cornish Mines Supplies' stand at 'State 69', demonstrating the latest range of domestic heaters. (HP)

St Austell Fire Station's open day, c.1970. The first such open day had taken place on 28 September 1967 at the fire station in Bodmin Road. (CCFB)

By the end of the period the Classic Theatre was staging popular live performances, including the 'Hip-Hip-Away Show'. (AD)

The line-up included Nite People, Vanity Fare and Marmalade. (AD)

Chapter Eight

THE CLAY COUNTRY AND HINTERLAND

Higher Ninestones engine house with its unusual square chimney. Nearby, during the early 1970s, a new road was cut through the clay works between Carluddon and Stenalees so that Penhale china-clay pit could be enlarged. (WhM)

A panoramic view of the clay country north of St Austell. In the foreground is Higher Ninestones, while at the top of the pit is the electricity substation at Carbean, next to the road decending to Carthew. Lower Ninestones is on the left. Carslake Cottages, now long gone, stand out on the horizon. Today the railway branch line to Gunheath, on the right, is an unmade road frequented by Land Rovers from the works. (IM)

Screda Relay Station dominates the skyline just north of the town. At over 213 metres (700 ft) above sea level the crest of the hill, known locally as 'Look Out', provides a vantage point for miles around. Here engineers are seen fixing a new bowl to the mast on 27 March 1962. Of course, since then many more have sprouted from it. (GE)

THE CLAY COUNTRY AND HINTERLAND

Nanpean Wharf on 16 June 1958. (WhM)

The village of Stenalees in 1962, dominated by the white pyramids of the china-clay industry – the tall tip on the right and the dries form Imperial's clay works. Beyond the wall is the cemetery at Treverbyn, with the cemetery chapel on the left. In her book *Vanishing Cornwall*, first published in 1967, Daphne du Maurier noted: 'Bugle, Stenalees, Foxhole, Nanpean, Treviscoe, St Stephen's-in-Brannel, St Dennis, these were villages or scattered hamlets once, and have developed solely on account of china-clay, housing the majority of its workers.' (IM)

Right: Greensplat engine house, with the lower winding house on the right, photographed on 29 May 1958. The driver checked the incline behind him through a mirror and by the use of an indicator that looked like a clock dial. (IM)

Below: The engine house at the Greensplat works of F.W. Berk. The beam engine was the last to work commercially in Cornwall and operated until February 1959, when engine man Arthur Hancock shut it down for the last time. It was eventually rescued and taken to Poldark Mine near Helston in 1972–3. (IM)

Trethosa china-clay pit, showing a hand-controlled monitor for washing clay from the pit face. Automatic monitors were introduced in 1962–3 and were hydraulically operated. A Ruston Bucyrus 22-RB crane is loading overburden onto a dumper. (IM)

Looking south across Penhale china-clay works towards the coast. Black Head can be seen above the cloud of smoke. The town itself is hidden beneath the brow of the hill. Apart from Great Treverbyn sky tip, which still dominates the skyline above the town, the view has greatly altered since this photograph was taken – an interesting comparison can be made from Caerloggas Downs, formerly Singlerose sand tip, open to the public since 1998. It provides a commanding view of the area, being 277 metres (910 ft) above sea level. (IM)

Blackpool pit in 1962. It was one of E.C.L.P.'s biggest and most productive pits. (IM)

Another view of Blackpool china-clay works. The inclines can be seen clearly, while on the right a monitor is firing a jet of water at the rock-face. (IM)

Looking down the incline into a china-clay pit. A monitor is at work on the clay face. In 1964 annual output by E.C.L.P. reached 2,007,000 tonnes. (IM)

An unfortunate accident at Treviscoe in 1962 when the steel fabrication for a new building collapsed. (IM)

Meledor china-clay works, St Stephen. The lorry gives a sense of scale to the scene. (IM)

THE CLAY COUNTRY AND HINTERLAND

From Blackpool china-clay works, looking across refining tanks towards the town, St Austell Bay and Gribbin Head. In the centre of the picture are old tips at Halvigan above Gover Valley. (IM)

Looking across fields towards Burngullow and Blackpool china-clay works. The photograph pre-dates the construction of the tall clay silos that now dominate the scene, as well as residential developments at Trewoon as the town grows westward. Although hidden from view, the A3058 road to St Stephen runs across the picture beneath the closest sand tip. (IM)

Wheal Remfry Brickworks, showing the remains of a beehive kiln. The last brickworks in the area closed in 1977. (IM)

Virginia water-wheel at Fal Valley near St Stephen, built by Harvey & Co. of Hayle. Technological advances had made it redundant, but plans have since been made to restore it. (IM)

Kernick china-clay pit, photographed in July 1952. The lorries at the bottom of the incline are dwarfed by the scale of the excavations. The first mechanical sand classifiers were introduced by E.C.L.P. at Kernick pit in 1958. (IM)

Holding tanks at Goverseth refining plant above Nanpean. In the background, beyond the building in the centre, is Rostowrack china-clay works and to its left Fal Valley, and Kernick by the diagonal stanchion. (IM)

THE CLAY COUNTRY AND HINTERLAND

Gunheath china-clay pit in 1960. The picture illustrates changing production methods, with abandoned inclines and engine houses clearly visible, while domestic houses also nestle in this lunar landscape. (IM)

Filter-press decks at one of the drying plants. (IM)

Batteries of filter presses. (IM)

After the clay has been allowed to thicken in settling tanks it is squeezed in these filter presses to create solid cakes of china clay. Today the cast-iron plates have been replaced by ones formed from polypropylene. Circular plate presses and tube presses have also been developed since this picture was taken. (IM)

A china-stone quarry run by E.C.L.P. A tramway can be seen running through the canyons to facilitate the removal of the rock. (IM)

The primary and secondary rock-crushing plants at Quarry Close between Nanpean and St Dennis that were used for processing china stone. (IM)

Another view of Quarry Close from the other side. (IM)

The crushing-plant conveyors at Quarry Close, with piles of crushed china stone in the foreground. (IM)

Chapter Nine
ONE CHRISTMAS EVE...

In compiling this book a superb collection of photographs came to light. They are unique insofar as they were all taken on a single day, Christmas Eve 1983, and have never before been published. The photographer, John Smith, spent a day in the town from dawn to past midnight capturing the sights and scenes, people and places within the exciting atmosphere that precedes Christmas Day. We have included a selection of these photographs in the final section of this book as, not only are they of interest in themselves, but also because they reveal how quickly things change. They remind us too of the importance of looking to the past in order to keep hold of the essential elements of the place in which we live.

Laden with Christmas presents, a last minute shopper walks past the Chinese restaurant at the back of Woolworth's.

Shoppers crowd in rainy Fore Street.

ONE CHRISTMAS EVE...

Fore Street looking east. The National Provincial building society had by now moved here from Church Street. Myners is now the Old Manor House in North Street, while the SWEB premises is currently ETS.

Above and below: Revellers in the White Hart.

ONE CHRISTMAS EVE...

We sell snuff!

A busy Fore Street looking west.

Men behaving badly outside the Queens Head.

Buskers outside the old Midland Bank.

ONE CHRISTMAS EVE...

Dedicated followers of fashion.

Outside Boots the Chemists, Fore Street.

Selling pasties in the street.

Fred Buscombe who sold Glanfield's pasties on Saturdays in the *Cornish Guardian* doorway.

ST AUSTELL – *The Golden Years*

St Austell Rotary Club's barrel organ raising money for the old people of the town.

Thorpe's electrical store is now a betting shop, while Alliance Building Society has become Alliance and Leicester.

ONE CHRISTMAS EVE...

Vicarage Hill, looking down towards the jewellers.

A makeshift Father Christmas grotto in the Market House.

Popular entertainment in the Town Centre was this showman's engine and roundabout.

The Cornwall Dance Centre provided entertainment of a more formal kind.

ONE CHRISTMAS EVE...

Del Monico's wine shop remains much the same today.

Fore Street: note the festive lighting.

Visionhire.

ONE CHRISTMAS EVE...

The General Wolfe.

Fore Street before pedestrianisation.

Holy Trinity Church.

ONE CHRISTMAS EVE...

Above and below: Worshippers arriving for the midnight service at Holy Trinity.

Christmas Eve live music – in a miner key!

ONE CHRISTMAS EVE...

Joe Matta, traffic warden.

Two policemen pose beside their Ford Cortina 'jam sandwich' in South Street.

Above and below: happy residents.

Left: WPC Bridget Branney

Tony McCameron, the last street cleaner in St Austell is seen here not long before the process was mechanised.

The White Hart.

Reg Haywood, Trophy Sports, High Cross Street.

ONE CHRISTMAS EVE...

Roy Dutch, proprietor of Camera Corner in East Hill.

David Del Monico.

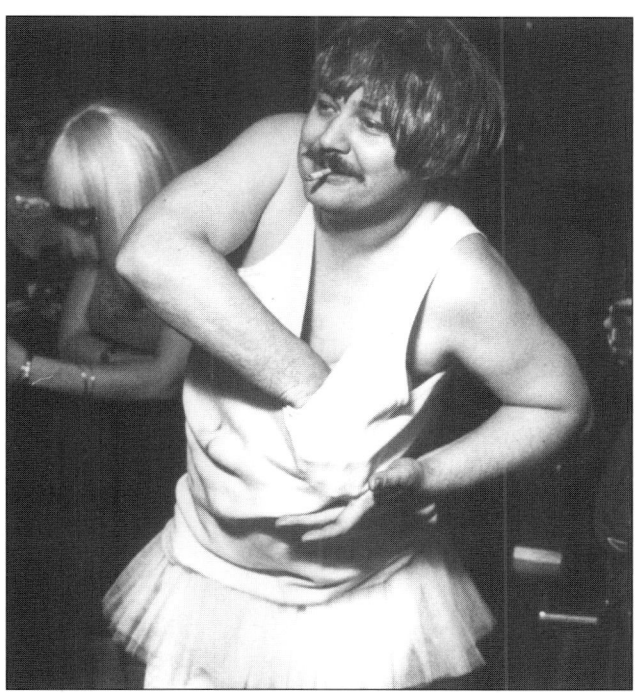

"Hold on, it's here somewhere!"

Dave Rowe, who ran the Polgooth Inn.

ONE CHRISTMAS EVE...

Busking it outside the Midland Bank.

Party time at the Carlyon Arms, better known as the 'Sandy Pub'.

ONE CHRISTMAS EVE...

Anonymous smile.

Milko!

ST AUSTELL – *The Golden Years*

Just singing in the rain…

ONE CHRISTMAS EVE...

Peter Bray, proprietor Bray & Sons, men's outfitters and camping stores, Market House.

Too much choice.

More happy shoppers, Fore Street.

A quiet word in the General Wolfe.

Reg Haywood, among his trophies.

Peter Goodman, newsagent and tobacconist.

ONE CHRISTMAS EVE...

John Cooksley and Stan Wallace.

The last of the poultry orders for another Christmas.

Christine Walker who ran the White Hart with David her husband.

The off-license in Market Street was busy. This shop no longer exists.

ONE CHRISTMAS EVE...

Barlows Cycles, Market House.

David and Ada Slinger, proprietors of Barlows Cycles.

Roy Dutch raises his glass to a 'Snappy Christmas'!

Candy.

ONE CHRISTMAS EVE...

Frying tonight.

'Local Pheasants £5.50 a brace.'

Tony takes a break from sweeping Fore Street.

A hectic day for W.H. Smith.

ONE CHRISTMAS EVE...

Currys.

Alan Brown, Manager of Currys.

Making ready for the January sales.